D1631917

GREATEST

Scouse One-Liners

GREATEST

Scouse
One-
Liners

Ian Black

BLACK & WHITE PUBLISHING

First published 2013
by Black & White Publishing Ltd
29 Ocean Drive, Edinburgh EH6 6JL

1 3 5 7 9 10 8 6 4 2   13 14 15 16

ISBN 978 1 84502 490 1

A CIP catalogue record for this book is available
from the British Library.

Typeset by RefineCatch Limited, Bungay
Printed and bound in Poland
www.hussarbooks.pl

A Scouse Two-Liner

Rumours that after the match the Everton squad was seen successfully seducing young women in a nightclub with one-liners have been completely refuted by this month's manager, Roberto Martinez.

He states: 'I find it totally preposterous to suggest that any of our players could make a successful pass to, or at, anyone.'

Scouse Questions

Yer said 'no' to drugs, did yer? They wern't listenin, weer they?

Yeh, sure, I'd like ter elp yer out, whurr did yer come in?

Are yer into casual sex,
or should I dress up?

10,000,000 sperm an yew were the fastest?

Wid enough force, pigs fly
ol ri. Want ter join them?

Dyer still love nature, la, despite what it did ter yer?

Dyer want folk ter accept yer as ye are or dyer want them ter like yer?

Wots yer problem, wack? I'm bettin its ard ter pronounce.

I'm busy ri now. Can I ignore yer some other time?

Wot am I, ere? Flypaper for freaks, soft lad?

Nobody likes yer,
surely yer remember?

Yew av de right to remain silent, but yer don av de ability, do yer?

An which dwarf are yew?

Scouse Threats
and Insults

Make yer name Walker, wack.
Ere's yer at, wur's de urry?

If yer can't fight, wur a big at.
Yew cudden punch an ole
in a wet *Echo*.

Erz owl scatter-the-cash.
E's thah tight e terns the gas
off ter tern the bacon over.

Gerroff an iron yer face,
yer old biddy.

De last thing I wanna do is hurt yer. But it's still on me list.

Hey, little un. Yer know wot?
When it rains, you'll be the
last ter know.

I thought I saw yer name on a loaf terday, but when I looked closer it said 'thick *cut*'.

Heh, divvy, yerve got a face like an orse in the uff.

Tha chin of yers looks like
a docker's kneecap.

When they wur givin out
bellies you jumped the queue
cos yer thought they said
jellies, didn't yer, yer fat wap?

Yer feet are so big, dat if yer trew a shoe in the Mersey it ud be an azard ter shippin.

Wi dose ears yer look like a taxi wid de doors open.

Cheer up, soft lad, yerve a
face like a wet Whit weekend.

Yer berd's dat ugly, she'd frighten a sailor off a raft.

If yer wur a McDonald's snack yer would be a Fillet O' Fish . . . Nobody likes yer, but yer always there.

WOT THE ELL IS THAT
ON YER NECK? Aw, ri,
it's just yer ead.

Don lewk at me tha way or I'll split yer in three ole affs.

Yer teeth ur like the Ten Commandments: all broken.

Instant beaut.
Just add alcohol.

Tesco needs yer.
Dey've run out ov stupid.

I'd call yer a fanny, kidder, but yer seem ter lack warmth and depth.

Here's a pound, divvy,
gerroff an buy yerself a life.

Pick a window,
wack, yer leavin.

If I agreed wid yer
we'd both be wrong.

I didn't say it was your fault,
I said I was blamin yer.

Im, e thinks Johnny Cash is wot it costs fer condoms.

Yer teeth ur like a row ov bombies – since 1944.

Hay yew, wen dey wer givin out brains yew tort dey said trains and yeh wern't goin anywhere.

I'd like ter see things from
your point ov view but I
can't seem to get me ead
that far up me arse.

I don ave an attitude problem.
Yew've got a perception
problem.

You, la, are a waste ov two billion years ov evolution.

If yer looking for sympathy, la, yew'll find it in the dictionary between 'shit' an 'syphilis'.

If I wanted ter ear from an arseole I would've farted.

Everybody as the right to
be stupid, but yer abusing
the privilege.

Yer multi-talented, so yer are.
Yer can talk and piss me off
at the same time.

Yew've got more issues
than the *Echo.*

Hay you, yer, you,
the oxygen thief.

Don annoy me. I'm running out ov places ter put bodies.

When dey put teeth in your gob, dey spoiled a perfectly good arse.

Just because you've gorra
prick don't mean yer av
ter act like one.

Yer a spherical arsehole.
No matter which way
yer tern, yer an arsehole
from every angle.

Wit a face like yours, every day is Halloween.

I'd like ter leave yer wid one tort, but I'm not sure yew've got anywer ter purr it.

La, I could eat a bowl ov
alphabet soup an shite a
better argument than tha.

Yer just not yerself today. I noticed the improvement.

Be yerself?
Bad advice fer you, son.

I don know wot makes yer
tha stupid, burrit's werkin.

If wot yer don know
can't hurt yer, den you,
boy, ur invulnerable.

If yer brain was chocolate
it wooden fill a Smartie.

Save yer breath, meff,
yew'll need it ter blow up
yer girlfriend later.

Yew've got tha many slates missin yer due a Council grant.

Don't play stupid with me –
I'm better at it.

Yer would be out yer depth
in a car park puddle.

If yer were any stupider, we'd
av ter water yer twice a week.

If shite was music, yew wid
de ead like a jarraworms,
you'd be an orchestra.

Darrell do yer. Calm yerself
down, la, or Paddy ere
will show yer de 'knife in
the eejit' trick.

I'd bet money that when yer stayed at Michael Jackson's as a kid, he made yer sleep in yer own bed.

Act soft, la, and I'll
buy yer a coalyard.

Whatever kind of lewk yer
were goin for, yer missed.

Scouse Names

Dey call im Compass – is nose goes North an is ears go South.

Baker over ther? The wife and kids are gone. Now it's only im an is tart.

De Balloon is always sayin:
'Don let me down.'

E always makes a bolt fer the door when it's is round – dat's why they call im Blacksmith.

The Depth Charge,
e's always after a sub.

Dey call im De Ghost –
always moanin.

Arpic? e's clean roun de bend.

The Lame Kangaroo?
E asnt ad a jump in years.

Whenever Jigsaw is asked ter
do sumtin e goes ter pieces.

Scouse Philosophy

Don walk behind me, for I may not lead. Don walk ahead of me, for I may not follow. Don walk beside me, either. Jus boogaroff, would yer?

One big voddy, two big voddy,
three big voddy, more.
Four big voddy, five big voddy,
six big voddy, floor.

Shame about im.
E's marchin ter the beat
ov a different kettle ov fish.

Don take life so seriously,
kidder. It isn't permanent –
specially if it's yours.

I feel as if I've gorra face
like a dollop ov mortal sins.

Just say no. *Den* negotiate.

Wot's for yer won't go past yer, and yer deserve it, whopper.

If yer don care where yer are,
then yer not lost.

In Crocky, it's sad ow ole famlies ur torn apart by simple things, like a pack ov wild dogs.

I've got plenty ov talent
and vision an that.
I just don give a shit.

I'd crawl a million miles across broken glass ter kiss the exhaust ov the van tha took er dirty knickers ter the laundry.

I've got de wisdom ov youth,
and de energy ov old age.

God must love stupid people.
E made you an millions
like yer.

Scouse Insults to Men

E's not stupid – it's kinda like e's possessed by a retarded ghost.

E's the kinda fella that yer could use as a blueprint to build an eejit.

If e was my dog, I'd shave
his arse and teach him
to walk backwards.

Those scars ov is? A lifetime
ov playin Tick wi atchets.

E's gorra face like a
forty-shilling piss pot –
pure white, but all chipped.

De only big thing abou im is is ears – he looks like an elephant wit the wind behind im.

Yeh, shame. His mam couldn breastfeed im – e wis cerdling the milk.

Im? he's suffering
from bottle fatigue.

Fat? E can sing a duet on is own.

Im! A brass once told
im she ad an eadache.

My Peter and sex?
Dis morning I used im
ter time an egg.

Im, e's gorran IQ ov two.
It takes three ter grunt.

I keep thinkin, if e talks
enough, someday e'll say
somethin intelligent.
Am I oldin me breath? No.

My man is no good at sex,
but e's thinkin ov takin
it up as an obby.

I thought abou im all day today. I was at the zoo.

I've ad a really good time,
but this wern't it.

My Peter is good lookin,
de trouble is, is teeth are
brighter than e is.

I'll never forget the first time I met him. Christ knows I keep tryin.

E's so narrow-minded that when e walks is earrins knock together.

My Tommy? E's got undreds ov well-wishers. Everybody wants to throw him down one.

Sorry mate, I carn't put
small objects in me mout
or I'll choke.

Im? The only place he's ever invited to is outside.

A shag? How about never, yew prick?

I'll try being nicer if yez
try bein better lookin,
divvy. Do one.

My Mick? You could use
his prick to stitch tapestry
if it wern't attached.

Im? E makes The Elephant
Man look like Mr Universe.

Listen, divvy, when yew were born, they slung the kid and kept the afterbirth.

Scouse Insults
to Women

When she undresses,
yer can ear the Lycra
breathe a sigh ov relief.

She's so ugly she tried
to take a bath and the
water jumped out.

She's cured undreds
ov Peepin Toms.

She's andled more
balls than Doni.

She's bin cocked more times
than Elmer Fudd's shotgun.

She's seen more
stiffs than Quincy.

She's so ugly, she'd frighten a monkey out ov a banana tree.

She's gorra face that could
make an onion cry.

She's gorra face on her that would drive rats from a barn.

She's got more chins than
a Chinese phone book.

She's seen more Jap's eyes
than an Oriental optician.

It's like shaggin the sleeve off
a wizard's cloak.

She's so bandy, she couldn
stop a pig in an alley.

When she sucks a lemon,
the lemon pulls a face.

She's gorran arse like
a bag ov washin.

She sweats like a dog in a
Chinese restaurant.

She's gorra face like a stuntman's knee.

It's like shaggin
a pail ov water.

She's seen more cock
ends than weekends.

She's so ugly not even a
sniper would take er out.

She's done more lengths
than Duncan Goodhew.

Even the tide wooden
take er out.

She's got more fingerprints
on er than Scotland Yard.

She's ad more seamen
than the docks.

She's got a mout on er like a
camel eating toast.

She's called De Olympic Torch
– she never goes out.

The finest woman that
ever walked the streets.